To: Jessie & Mallory

From: Aunt Maggie

Penguins and Polar Bears
ANIMALS OF THE ICE AND SNOW

Two Adélie penguins slide across the snow.

by Sandra Lee Crow

BOOKS FOR YOUNG EXPLORERS
NATIONAL GEOGRAPHIC SOCIETY

Everywhere you look there is ice. It floats on the ocean around Antarctica, the coldest place on earth. You can see the land and the cold sea around it at the bottom of the globe. In this frozen world live six kinds of penguins. Can you find the two penguins crossing the ice? Adélie penguins stand on an iceberg.

South Pole

Emperor

Chinstrap

King

You can tell penguins apart
by the markings on their heads.

Adélie

Gentoo

Macaroni penguins have long orange feathers on top
of their heads. All penguins have nearly the same shape.
They have smooth, rounded bodies. A thick layer of fat
helps them stay warm. All penguins have black-and-white
patterns that help hide them in the water. From below,
their white bellies are hard to see against the light sky.
Seen from above, their black backs blend with the water.

Macaroni

Leaping and diving like dolphins, Adélie penguins speed through the sea. They rise from the water every few seconds to breathe. Penguins are birds, but they cannot fly. They swim, using their wings as paddles and steering with their legs. Their feathers fit tightly together and help keep their bodies warm and dry.

Like a little rocket, an Adélie penguin shoots out of the sea. Another lands. It digs its toes into the ice and stops.

Penguins spend most of their lives in the water. There they catch and eat fish and other animals called squid and krill. In the sea, penguins must always watch for danger. These Adélies standing on an iceberg are safe. Nearby, a leopard seal swims in the cold water. Any bird that jumps in now could become the seal's next meal.

Chinstrap penguins ride
the waves onto a sandy beach.
When the sea ice breaks up
in spring, thousands of penguins
come ashore. Most return
to the same place every year.
There they mate and lay eggs.

The males arrive first and wait for
the females. Sometimes males
fight for their own spot of ground.
The birds greet their mates
by waving their flippers
and raising their bills.

A male gentoo penguin offers his mate a rock for their nest. He also gathers feathers, bones, and anything else he can move. Another gentoo is turning its eggs. Most kinds of penguins have two eggs at a time. The parents take turns keeping them warm.

Largest of all penguins, emperors are nearly as tall as a five-year-old child. Each of these males carries an egg on his feet, hidden under a fold of skin. A female emperor lays one egg in the middle of winter, then goes back to sea to eat. The male keeps the egg warm. She returns two months later, as her chick hatches.

Adélie penguins watch a brown bird called a skua as it circles overhead. Skuas eat penguin eggs and chicks. If the skua comes too close, the adult penguins will smack it with their flippers. Young chicks need a lot of care. One fluffy chick, two weeks old, snuggles beside its parent.

A chick is always hungry. Its parents bring it krill in their throats.
The muddy chick pushes its head into the parent's mouth to eat the food.

Thousands of king penguins stand side by side in the mud. Which ones are the chicks? They are the ones with soft brown coats of down. Chicks are born in summer and stay near their parents. After a few weeks, they gather in groups called nurseries. This helps keep them warm and safe.

Bit by bit, the chicks lose their fluffy feathers. Adult feathers have grown in under the down. These feathers will keep the birds dry. Now the penguins can swim and find their own food at sea.

Taking giant steps, a polar bear
moves silently over the snow.
This animal is twice as large as
a lion or a tiger. The polar bear
lives in the Arctic, at the other
end of the earth from penguins.

Like penguins, polar bears
have a thick layer of fat, called
blubber, under their skin.
Their black skin is covered by
soft white underfur and
a thick coat of outer hairs.
In cold wind or in icy water,
polar bears stay warm.

Dripping wet, a polar bear climbs onto the ice. Like dogs,
polar bears dry off by shaking the water from their hair.
They also swim like dogs, paddling with their front paws.
Polar bears hunt seals on the ice that floats on the Arctic Ocean.
Look for this ocean surrounded by land at the top of the globe.

North Pole

In some places, the sea ice melts in summer and polar bears come to shore. Three cubs tag along with their mother. They were born in a snow-covered den in winter. At birth, they could not see or hear, and had almost no hair. They grew fast by drinking their mother's milk. Now six months old, the cubs follow their mother everywhere.

By their second summer, cubs are nearly as big as their mother. They are learning how to hunt. On land, they eat grass and berries. They may take eggs from a duck's nest. Sometimes they catch a ground squirrel. But this may not be enough food for the big bears. They live mainly off their body fat until they can hunt seals again.

Arctic ground squirrel

King eider ducks

The bears become restless and hungry by the end of a summer on land. They gather in groups on the shore. They are waiting for the sea to freeze so they can go hunt for seals. Growling at each other, the bears roll and tumble. Their battles are mostly play.

After playing all day, a bear takes time out to rest. It sticks its face into the icy water and cools off.

The sea is beginning to freeze.
Polar bears will soon head out.
Each usually hunts alone. It may
wait patiently over a hole in the ice.
The bear will strike like lightning if
a seal pokes its head up to breathe.

The bear might also sneak up on
a seal as it rests in the sun. The bear
is hard to see on the snow. It is also
hard to hear. Fur under its paws
softens the sounds of its steps.

With summer over, the time has
almost come for the bear to leave.
One day the bear is on shore.
The next day it will be gone,
back to its home on the ice.

Ringed seal

Published by The National Geographic Society, Washington, D. C.
Gilbert M. Grosvenor, *President*
Melvin M. Payne, *Chairman of the Board*
Owen R. Anderson, *Executive Vice President*
Robert L. Breeden, *Vice President, Publications and Educational Media*

Prepared by The Special Publications Division
Donald J. Crump, *Director*
Philip B. Silcott, *Associate Director*
William L. Allen, *Assistant Director*

Staff for this book
Jane H. Buxton, *Managing Editor*
Karen G. Yee, *Picture Editor*
Jody Bolt, *Art Director*
Pamela J. Castaldi, *Designer*
Stephen J. Hubbard, *Researcher*
Artemis S. Lampathakis, *Illustrations Assistant*
Elizabeth Ann Brazerol, Dianne T. Craven, Carol Rocheleau
    Curtis, Mary Elizabeth Davis, Rosamund Garner,
    Virginia W. Hannasch, Cleo Petroff, Pamela Black Townsend,
    Virginia A. Williams, Eric Wilson, *Staff Assistants*

Engraving, Printing, and Product Manufacture
Robert W. Messer, *Manager*
George V. White, *Production Manager*
George J. Zeller, Jr., *Production Project Manager*
Mark R. Dunlevy, David V. Showers, Gregory Storer, *Assistant
    Production Managers;* Mary A. Bennett, *Production Assistant;*
    Julia F. Warner, *Production Staff Assistant*

Consultants
Lynda Bush, *Reading Consultant*
Lila Bishop, *Educational Consultant*
Steven C. Amstrup, Polar Bear Project Leader, U. S. Fish and
    Wildlife Service, and Dr. David E. Murrish, Department of
    Biological Science, State University of New York,
    Scientific Consultants

Illustrations Credits
Art Wolfe (Cover, 4 upper right, 18 left, 28-29 both); Francisco Erize/Bruce
Coleman Inc. (1); Gregory G. Dimijian, M.D./The Nat'l Audubon Soc.
Coll./PR (2-3, 8); Robert Hernandez, National Geographic Staff (3 upper, 5,
13); Jen and Des Bartlett (4 upper left, 6-7, 11, 18 right, 27 right, 27 lower);
William R. Fraser (4 lower left); M. P. Kahl/The Nat'l Audubon Soc. Coll./PR
(4 top center); M. P. Kahl/DRK PHOTO (4 lower right, 17); Robert
Hernandez/The Nat'l Audubon Soc. Coll./PR (9, 12-13); Bruno J. Zehnder
(10-11); Doug Allan/OXFORD SCIENTIFIC FILMS (14-15); Roger Tory
Peterson/The Nat'l Audubon Soc. Coll./PR (16 upper); William R.
Curtsinger/The Nat'l Audubon Soc. Coll./PR (16 lower); George
Holton/The Nat'l Audubon Soc. Coll./PR (18-19); Ranulph Fiennes (20-21);
Dotte Larsen/Bruce Coleman Inc. (22-23); Miriam MacMillan (23 lower);
Wayne Lankinen (24-25); C. Sid Rucker (26-27); Fred Bruemmer (30 left);
MASTERFILE (30 right); Paul von Baich (31); Thor Larsen (32).

Library of Congress CIP Data
Crow, Sandra Lee, 1948-
    Penguins and polar bears.

    (Books for young explorers)
    Summary: Describes the physical characteristics and life cycle of two animals adapted for survival in
polar climates, the penguin at the Antarctic and the polar bear at the Arctic.
    1. Penguins — Juvenile literature. 2. Polar bear — Juvenile literature. [1. Penguins. 2. Polar bear]
I. Title. II. Series.
QL696.S473C76   1985   598.4'41   85-21461
    ISBN 0-87044-562-6 (regular edition)
    ISBN 0-87044-567-7 (library edition)

Footprints in the snow mark the path of a polar bear,
mighty hunter of the Arctic.

COVER: Two Adélie penguins huddle on an
iceberg. The best known penguins, Adélies look
like little men dressed up for an evening party.

MORE ABOUT Penguins and Polar Bears

What does a huge polar bear have in common with flightless seabirds called penguins? The answer, of course, is that both are animals of the polar regions.

The polar regions lie at the northernmost and southernmost points of the world. Both are regions of continuous cold. A look at a globe helps explain why (3, 23).* The earth is always tilted as it makes its annual journey around the sun. As a result, the sun does not strike the polar regions directly, even in summer.

The Arctic is mostly ocean, surrounded by the continents of North America, Europe, and Asia. Much of the ocean's surface is frozen year-round, with ice some eight to twelve feet thick. The ice constantly moves, sometimes breaking into ice floes—wide, floating slabs (22-23). Sea ice, or pack ice, is inhospitable to arctic land animals other than polar bears and their occasional scavenger companions, arctic foxes.

In the brief arctic summer, the treeless land called tundra bursts into life (26-27). Many birds migrate there. Herds of caribou graze on vegetation anchored in the top layer of soil. The land beneath, permafrost, stays permanently frozen.

The Antarctic, at the opposite end of the globe, is the coldest place on earth. The lowest recorded temperature there was -127°F. The desolate, frozen continent of Antarctica, which is nearly twice the size of Australia, is almost entirely covered by an ice sheet more than a mile thick. This continent has no trees and only a few plants. Experts estimate that Antarctica contains 70 percent of all the

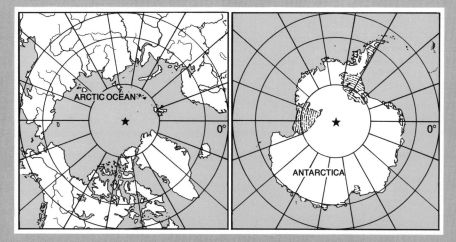

Polar maps reveal the Arctic and the Antarctic—one an ocean circled by continents, the other a continent surrounded by ocean—and help explain why their climates differ. The Arctic Ocean retains heat, moderating its climate. Antarctica's ice cap reflects heat, making it earth's coldest place.

snow and ice in the world, the result of 20 million years of accumulation.

Only the six hardiest penguin species can survive in the Antarctic (4-5). These include the four-foot-tall emperors; kings, slightly smaller than emperors; the orange-plumed macaronis, named for 18th-century dandies; gentoos, with crests of white; chinstraps, which have a narrow black line across their throats; and the most familiar of all, Adélies. The remaining 11 penguin species live predominantly above 60° South.

Polar bears and Antarctic penguins are completely at home in their environments. Both animals have a thick, insulating layer of blubber, and dense body coverings. The polar bear's oily, woolly undercoat is covered with long, transparent guard hairs that allow sunlight to reach and warm the bear's black skin (20-21). In a severe storm, a polar bear may dig a temporary den in a snowbank.

The penguin has numerous feathers. Some 300 feathers may grow in an area the size of a postage stamp. The oil-coated feathers are stiff and hooked at the tip, forming a tight, interlocking coat that traps air near the skin and helps keep the bird dry. Downlike fluff grows at the base of each feather, adding extra insulation. Penguins molt annually; during that time they must remain on land, for they would freeze in the water.

Animals of the polar regions find most of their food in the sea. Waters rich in nutrients support masses of tiny floating plants called phytoplankton. These, in turn, feed huge numbers of small animals such as the shrimplike krill. Krill, squid, and small fish form the staple diet of penguins and many seals.

Seals are the polar bear's chief prey. The bear, aided by its keen sense of smell, stalks seals as they nap on the ice (30), or snatches them from their

*Numbers in parentheses refer to pages in *Penguins and Polar Bears: Animals of the Ice and Snow.*

sea-ice birthing dens. Much of the time, seals live beneath several feet of ice. Each seal maintains several breathing holes, butting and chewing the ice to keep the holes open. The bear may wait by a hole for hours (30). Then suddenly, as the seal surfaces, the bear will strike with its massive paw and haul the seal out and eat it, sometimes consuming 100 pounds in one meal. In open water, seals can outswim polar bears.

In some places, the bears retreat to land in summer, scrounging for food and living off their fat reserves (24-29). Most polar bears follow the pack ice as it recedes.

Polar animals have evolved specialized ways of raising their young. Most Antarctic penguins nest in summer (12-13, 16-17). The parents cooperate in caring for the chicks. While one stands guard, the other hunts at sea. Upon returning, the parent regurgitates food that has been stored in its crop, a pouchlike portion of its throat. By the beginning

of autumn, the chicks have matured and are on their own.

Emperors (14-15) are the largest penguins, and their chicks take longer to mature. Because emperors lay their eggs earlier than other penguins do, the chicks have extra time to grow adult plumage by winter.

Each female emperor lays one egg out on the sea ice in winter, then heads to open water, sometimes 60 miles away, to feed. Her mate incubates the egg, carrying it on his feet for two months while enduring severe weather and living off his body fat. By the time the female returns and takes over the raising of the chick, the male has lost nearly half his body weight. He heads immediately to sea to feed.

Polar bear cubs are born in winter in the safety and warmth of a den. At birth, they are blind, deaf, and helpless. Their mother, living off her own body fat, sustains the cubs with her milk until they all emerge from the

den in spring. The mother, by then ravenous, leads the cubs onto the ice where she can catch seals. The mother teaches, guards, and feeds her cubs, sharing the prey she catches. After two years, the cubs hunt on their own.

Although the polar lands are distant, a globe and this book will provide an armchair visit. On the globe, note the differences between the polar regions. In this book, look for some of the features of these regions: tabletopped icebergs, shifting ice floes, tundra vegetation.

Locate photographs in this book that provide comparisons between penguins and polar bears—adaptations that help them stay warm, find food, and raise their young. Compare some of the animals' natural adaptations to their cold, wet environment with some of our inventions: down jackets, igloos, diver's wet suits, and waterproofing oil for boots.

Nothing can equal seeing the animals themselves. Some aquariums and zoos maintain exhibits of penguins and polar bears, which provide ideal sites for observation. These are the only places you will ever find penguins and polar bears closer than poles apart!

ADDITIONAL READING

Animals of the Antarctic, by Robert Burton. (N.Y., Abelard-Schuman, 1970). Ages 12 and up.

Life on Ice: How Animals Survive in the Arctic, by Seymour Simon. (N.Y., Franklin Watts, 1976). Ages 12 and up.

Lords of the Arctic: A Journey Among the Polar Bears, by Richard C. Davids. (N.Y., Macmillan, 1982). Family reading.

The Sea World Book of Penguins, by Frank S. Todd. (San Diego, Sea World Press, 1981). Ages 8 and up.

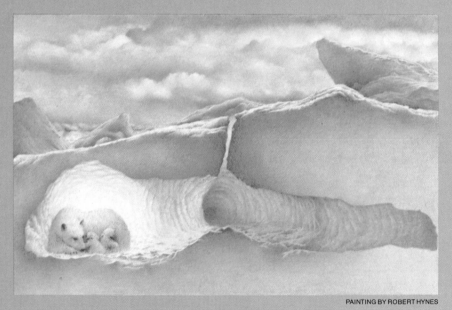

PAINTING BY ROBERT HYNES

A polar bear's maternity den shields mother and cubs from winter weather. The mother normally digs the den and enters it in October. Drifts soon cover the entrance. A narrow vent lets in fresh air. The cubs, usually twins, are born in December or January, weighing scarcely one pound each. They grow fast, suckling their mother's fat-rich milk. When shafts of light signal the onset of spring, the cubs, 20-pound youngsters, follow their mother outside.